Tara Vanhonacker .... Tara e.a. Kingdom of Thailand... OTP – CR – 351/17

Please find included several files with suspicious deaths of foreigners over the last 10 years in Thailand .... In my comments you will see a number of questions to be asked about each case ... Those questions could be asked by the Royal Thai Police, but they are not being asked ... because Thai society protects Thai criminals from their foreign victims ... and the Immigration Act is actually a legal instrument to make this situation possible ... it also shows the total disregard by Thai people for the lives of foreigners who have given them money and livelihood and houses for a very long time ...

This should be classified with the Crimes Against Humanity – Murder ... and it is organized because Thai people always tell foreigners that they should tell everyone in the world that there are no Thai murderers ...

On the last page you will find the probably crime being covered up and a possible motive ...

The Kundu File

A 59-year-old doctor from Calcutta died on holiday in Thailand moments after complaining of breathlessness while doing the Underwater Sea Walk, a guided marine stroll listed among the must-do activities during a trip to Koh Larn near Pattaya, Chon Buri province.

Indian gynaecologist Sukhendu Kumar Kundu, who used to run a nursing home at Behrampore in Murshidabad, had gone for the underwater walk on March 6 with a local tour operator, family members said on Tuesday.

Kundu was brought out of the water because of respiratory distress and taken to a government hospital in Pattaya but doctors had to declare him dead upon arrival. Doctors say Mr Kundu died of asphyxiation by drowning.

My comments :

Involuntary manslaughter by negligence …. insurance fraud

When you go on a trip underwater, the equipment should have been checked properly … in this case there was probably a malfunction in the diving equipment …

The lie used is to avoid being held responsible in litigation and with insurance companies …

If this were a Thai person … the cause of death would have been the above ...

Tara Vanhonacker .... Tara e.a. Kingdom of Thailand... OTP – CR – 351/17

Please find included several files with suspicious deaths of foreigners over the last 10 years in Thailand .... In my comments you will see a number of questions to be asked about each case ... Those questions could be asked by the Royal Thai Police, but they are not being asked ... because Thai society protects Thai criminals from their foreign victims ... and the Immigration Act is actually a legal instrument to make this situation possible ... it also shows the total disregard by Thai people for the lives of foreigners who have given them money and livelihood and houses for a very long time ...

This should be classified with the Crimes Against Humanity – Murder ... and it is organized because Thai people always tell foreigners that they should tell everyone in the world that there are no Thai murderers ...

On the last page you will find the probably crime being covered up and a possible motive ...

The Zhang File

Police are investigating the death of a 23-year-old Chinese woman whose body was found alone at a depth of 11 metres by a group of divers from another dive tour north of Phuket yesterday afternoon.

Divers from Khao Lak Scuba Adventures found the body of Zhang Lin near Koh Bon, off Kuraburi in Phang Nga, at about 14:30. Officials from the Similan National Park outpost in Kuraburi notified Marine Police that her body had been found at 19:00 last night.

Police said that, according to the divers who found her, Ms Zhang was floating face-down without her mouthpiece in place. They brought her body on board their dive boat, the Taisiri, and performed CPR in an attempt to revive her. However, Ms Zhang remained unresponsive.

A speedboat sped Ms Zhang ashore and she was rushed to Tai Muang Hospital, but doctors there said that she died at least six hours before her body was discovered. However, doctors also said they would request that an autopsy determine her cause of death. Photos show a cut over Ms Zhang's left eye and minor abrasions on her forehead.

Ms Zhang was with friends on a liveaboard dive tour on the MV Peterpan, operated by the Similan Seven Sea Club dive company based in Khao Lak, said Lt Col Chakri Maigumponsuth of the Phang Nga Marine Police "However, we are still investigating the nature of the incident," he said.

Police have notified the Chinese Embassy of Ms Zhang's death, he added.

My comments : Involuntary manslaughter by negligence …. insurance fraud

Accidents happen and again the accident … (a fall) is being portrayed as a mysterious death.

The probable lie used is to avoid being held responsible in litigation and with insurance companies …If this were a Thai person … the cause of death would have been the above …

Tara Vanhonacker .... Tara e.a. Kingdom of Thailand... OTP – CR – 351/17

Please find included several files with suspicious deaths of foreigners over the last 10 years in Thailand .... In my comments you will see a number of questions to be asked about each case ... Those questions could be asked by the Royal Thai Police, but they are not being asked ... because Thai society protects Thai criminals from their foreign victims ... and the Immigration Act is actually a legal instrument to make this situation possible ... it also shows the total disregard by Thai people for the lives of foreigners who have given them money and livelihood and houses for a very long time ...

This should be classified with the Crimes Against Humanity – Murder ... and it is organized because Thai people always tell foreigners that they should tell everyone in the world that there are no Thai murderers ...

On the last page you will find the probably crime being covered up and a possible motive ...

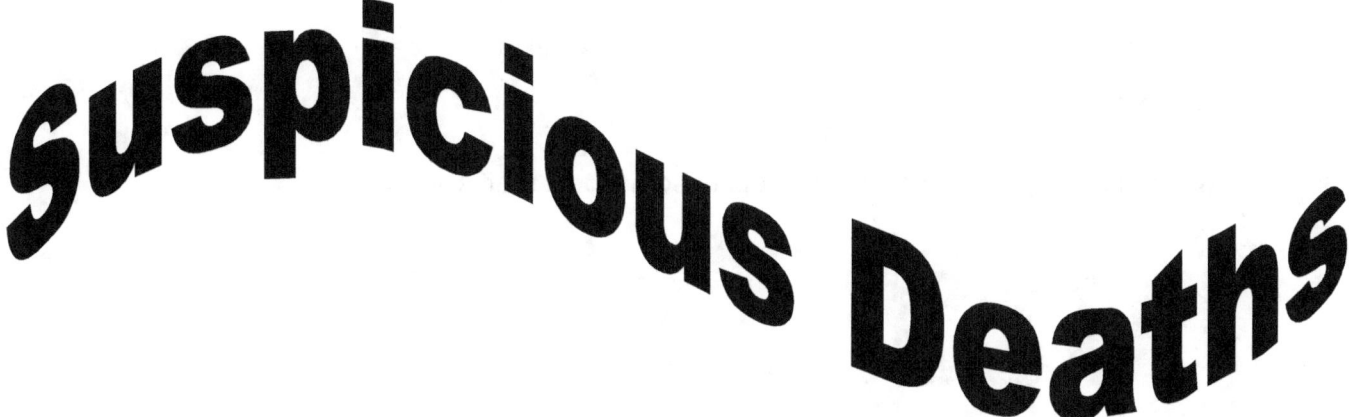

The Diaboula File

A 29-year-old Senegal human rights activist drowned whilst swimming in a water reservoir in Loei province on Tuesday morning.

Officers from Mueang Loei Provincial Police Station were informed of the incident at 10:20. The body of the male victim, who police later identified as Aliou Diaboula, was lying on the bottom of the lake in Huai Krating when officers and Sawang Rescue workers arrived at the accident site in Loei's Kok Thong district.

It took rescue divers more than six hours to recover the body. "When he was pulled out, he had already entered rigor mortis," Pol Maj Wanit Putwongdat said, adding that the investigation into the death of the Senegalese is still on-going.

Mr Diaboula had worked as an activist for several human rights organisations including: The International Youth Council, World Youth Alliance and Americans for Informed Democracy.

My comments : Murder

… and that of a human rights fighter … he probably upset some local maffia warlord …

Tara Vanhonacker .... Tara e.a. Kingdom of Thailand... OTP – CR – 351/17

Please find included several files with suspicious deaths of foreigners over the last 10 years in Thailand .... In my comments you will see a number of questions to be asked about each case ... Those questions could be asked by the Royal Thai Police, but they are not being asked ... because Thai society protects Thai criminals from their foreign victims ... and the Immigration Act is actually a legal instrument to make this situation possible ... it also shows the total disregard by Thai people for the lives of foreigners who have given them money and livelihood and houses for a very long time ...

This should be classified with the Crimes Against Humanity – Murder ... and it is organized because Thai people always tell foreigners that they should tell everyone in the world that there are no Thai murderers ...

On the last page you will find the probably crime being covered up and a possible motive ...

The Nordbo File

A Norwegian man was found dead next to the swimming pool of their house in Buriram province. Police consider the death to be an accident.

The body of Per Nordbø*, a 59-year-old man from Norway, was found by his 41-year-old wife on the morning of Friday, April 5. "Mrs Nordbø told us that he had already been dead when she saw him," an officer at Nang Rong Provincial Police Station confirmed.

Shortly later, officers and rescue workers arrived at the house at 113 Mu 13 in Nong Bot subdistrict of Buriram province. They briefly examined the body and discovered an injury: "Mr Nordbø had a bleeding laceration on his forehead that had created a small pool of blood on the ground," the officer noted, adding that this could have been caused by a fall. He died at least five hours earlier, police said.

Mrs Nordbø, the only witness, told police that her husband had left the house to catch some air because he had trouble falling asleep. "This was at around 1:00, she told us." When she woke up and went to the back of the house, she found Mr Nordbø laying dead next to the swimming pool and realised that he had died already.

The Thai newspaper Khaosod where the accident was published quoted police who assumed that "Mr Nordbø had suffered a shock and drowned". However, it was not explained how he could have drowned when his body was found outside of the pool. According to his wife, Mr Nordbø also suffered from a series health conditions that police did not elaborate any further.

* This name has been transliterated from Thai and might not be accurate.

My comments : Suspicious manslaughter

Did he drown, did he die from a hit to the head , did he fall ... what health conditions .... there are just no real and clear answers ....

Tara Vanhonacker .... Tara e.a. Kingdom of Thailand... OTP – CR – 351/17

Please find included several files with suspicious deaths of foreigners over the last 10 years in Thailand .... In my comments you will see a number of questions to be asked about each case ... Those questions could be asked by the Royal Thai Police, but they are not being asked ... because Thai society protects Thai criminals from their foreign victims ... and the Immigration Act is actually a legal instrument to make this situation possible ... it also shows the total disregard by Thai people for the lives of foreigners who have given them money and livelihood and houses for a very long time ...

This should be classified with the Crimes Against Humanity – Murder ... and it is organized because Thai people always tell foreigners that they should tell everyone in the world that there are no Thai murderers ...

On the last page you will find the probably crime being covered up and a possible motive ...

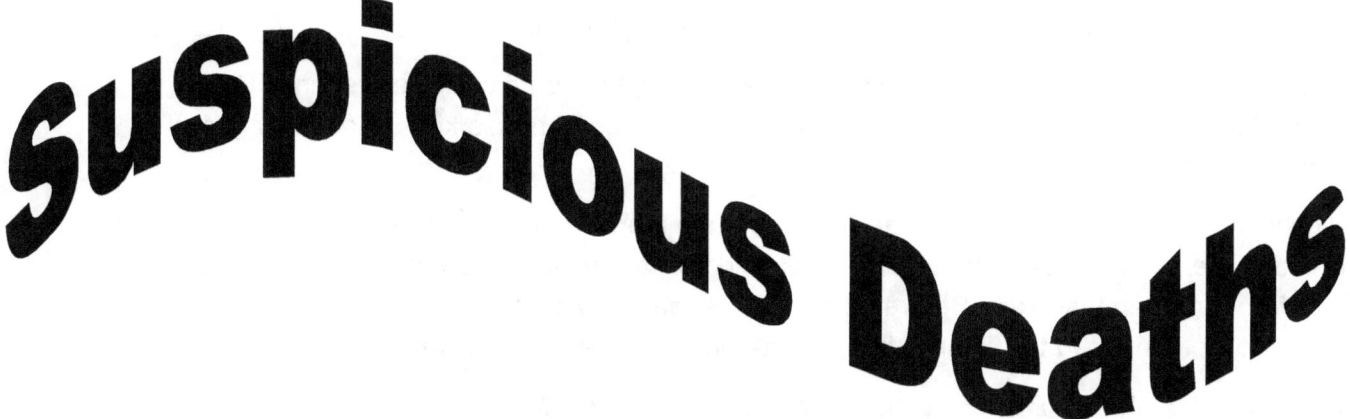

The David File

Police in Phitsanulok province continue to puzzle over the death of an elderly British man whose body was found in Nam River on Thursday morning.

Residents of the Nai Mueang subdistrict discovered the body floating on the river close to Wat Tha Maprang temple at around 09:30, Pol Capt Anuwad Watanagarun of Mueang Phitsanulok Provincial Police Station said. Police later identified him as 74-year-old Trevor Roberts David from England.

Volunteers of the Kawpab Rescue Association took his body to a nearby pier to allow a doctor from Naresuan University Hospital to examine it more closely.

Pol Capt Anuwad told reporters at Phitsanulok Hotnews, "Mr David was fully dressed wearing black trousers, a white shirt and shoes. We did not find any injuries or bruises on his body." The doctor on-the-scene estimated that Mr David had been dead for two to four hours.

Police checked his pockets and found a driving licence bearing his name transliterated into Thai. "We also found 2640 baht in cash, a watch, a car key and a bunch of house keys," said acting lead investigator, Pol Capt Anuwad.

While police were examining the body on the pier, a woman identifing herself as Mr David's sister-in-law arrived at the scene. Puangtong Nuanjan, 59, told police the victim had been living in Phitsanulok for more than ten years. Before retiring, he reportedly worked as an English teacher in the province. Police confirmed this information in a statement published later that day.

"Ms Puangtong told us that Mr David usually stayed at home, 999/11 Mu 3 in the Aranyik subdistrict and only occasionally went out to visit his friends who lived nearby." Police quoted Ms Puangtong as last seeing the victim alive when she was visiting her sister on Tuesday and noticed nothing unusual.

Police contacted the victim's wife, Bratueang David, to notify her of her husband's death. She was unaware of where he was or the location of his car. The police plan to question her further and determine the exact cause of death. At this early stage, they suspect Mr David drowned.

http://www.dailymail.co.uk/news/article-4500158/Retired-teacher-kills-Thailand-Pound-fall.html

Retired teacher, 74, 'kills himself in Thailand after fall in value of the Pound meant his pension was worth less and sparked arguments with his wife'
Trevor Roberts was found dead in a river in Phitsanulok, 300 miles from Bangkok
His wife told detectives that he had been complaining about his British pension
The 74-year-old's body was pulled from the Nan River in Phitsanulok on Thursday
British ex-pats have seen an eight per cent drop in sterling against Thai baht

Police in Thailand are trying to establish if a retired British teacher committed suicide because he was receiving lower pension payments.
Trevor Roberts was found dead in the Nan River in Phitsanulok, 300 miles north of Bangkok on Thursday.
Police were told by the 74-year-old's Thai wife that he had been complaining about his British pension, leading officers to consider whether this could be the reason for his death.

His body was pulled from the river about two hours after he was believed to have drowned - but police could find no immediate reason why he was in the water.

A former language teacher at a college in the Phitsanulok area, Mr Roberts had been living in the town for some 10 years and had recently been receiving a UK pension.

His original home town in the UK has not yet been revealed by police.

His sister-in-law, Phuangthong Nuanjan, has told police that Mr Roberts and his wife had been arguing lately because he was receiving less pension money than before due to changes in the way it was paid.

Although there have been no changes to British pensions, UK citizens living abroad have been hit by a fall in the value of the pound, causing many to suffer such heavy losses that they have even been considering returning home.

In Thailand, British ex-pats have suffered an eight per cent drop in sterling against the Thai baht.

As police try to establish whether Mr Roberts' death was the result of suicide because of his pension drop, an accident, or foul play, suicide was emerging as the most likely cause.

In his pocket police found his driving licence, 2,640 Thai baht (£59) and keys.

He was wearing a watch and also carried an appointment card for a visit to the town hospital.

Police who spoke to Mr Robert's wife, Pratheuang Roberts, were told that just two days earlier he had said he wanted to die, but she had thought nothing of it at the time.

As plans were being made for an autopsy, police were continuing to investigate the reason for the Briton's death.

My comments : Manslaughter

Manslaughter

Tara Vanhonacker …. Tara e.a. Kingdom of Thailand… OTP – CR – 351/17

Please find included several files with suspicious deaths of foreigners over the last 10 years in Thailand …. In my comments you will see a number of questions to be asked about each case … Those questions could be asked by the Royal Thai Police, but they are not being asked … because Thai society protects Thai criminals from their foreign victims … and the Immigration Act is actually a legal instrument to make this situation possible … it also shows the total disregard by Thai people for the lives of foreigners who have given them money and livelihood and houses for a very long time …

This should be classified with the Crimes Against Humanity – Murder … and it is organized because Thai people always tell foreigners that they should tell everyone in the world that there are no Thai murderers …

On the last page you will find the probably crime being covered up and a possible motive …

Taksamol Aobaom

Thailand is among the world's most dangerous countries in which to oppose powerful interests that profit from coal plants, toxic waste dumping, land grabs or illegal logging. Some 60 people who spoke out on these issues have been killed over the past 20 years, although few perpetrators have been prosecuted in a culture in which powerful people have the last word and professional killers are easy to find.

A 2014 report by the environmental watchdog group Global Witness ranked Thailand as the eighth most dangerous country in which to defend land and environmental rights. It is the second most dangerous country in Asia, after the Philippines.

The killings often involve small-scale conflicts in remote areas, and issues that might seem too narrow to carry assassination as a penalty. Few of them have received national coverage, and few of the names of those killed are widely known.

Portraits of 37 of these largely obscure victims comprise a new project by the Bangkok-based photographer Luke Duggleby and were exhibited this month in Geneva, timed to coincide with a United Nations Human Rights Council review of Thailand's human rights record.
"It is vital, for the victims and the families, that their fight and their death should not be forgotten and left unrecognized," Mr. Duggleby said in a statement accompanying his portfolio.

The question was how to present them. The victims were dead, or in a few cases had been abducted and disappeared. The only records in some cases were in the memories of families and in the portraits they kept of their relatives, sometimes in a frame on the wall, sometimes at a Buddhist altar.

It was these photographs that inspired the concept of his project: to place and photograph a portrait of the victim at the site of the murder or abduction. The result is a surprisingly moving set of photographs, mostly expressionless faces in formal photographs looking out from a field, a forest or rubber plantation or a roadside. In one case, the family had only an identification card picture, so Mr. Duggleby photographed and printed it to place at the scene.
The silent portraits, looking small and vulnerable in their settings, seem like tiny, passive missives from the victims, looking back at the viewer from the scene of their last terrifying moments.

In this way, in a very different context and with a very different aesthetic, they share a hollow resonance with the well-known black-and-white portraits of the dead that cover the walls of Tuol Sleng in Cambodia, the former prison where thousands of people were photographed before being tortured and killed.

Tallying the disparate, barely reported killings in Thailand has been difficult, and the first comprehensive list has only recently been compiled by Protection International, a human rights nongovernmental organization. One of its members, Pranom Somwong, worked with Mr. Duggleby in researching many of the cases.

For more than a year, Mr. Duggleby, who speaks fluent Thai, traveled with a Thai assistant throughout the country, covering by his calculation 10,000 kilometers, or more than 6,000 miles. He said he took great care not to endanger people or to make a situation worse.

Some of the disputes and threats remained real; in some cases other people had stepped forward to continue the resistance. One victim, for example, Chai Boonthonglek, 61, who was shot dead on Feb. 11, 2015, was the fourth member of his community to be murdered in five years during a dispute over land rights with a palm-oil company.

"The most important thing was the safety of the villagers," Mr. Duggleby said. "We made our presence very quiet and very quick. I'd talk to them, spend a few hours with them, finish and drive on to the next place."

P
h
o
t
o

They were, in general, well received, and were guided to the place of the killing. In some cases, he said, it was too dangerous or sensitive to meet the family, so they simply talked by telephone, determined the site of the killing, and with the family's permission took an image from the Internet.

In a country that, particularly in rural areas, is governed less by the rule of law than by impunity, the killers and the powerful forces behind them usually walk free.

"In more than one case the assassin still lives in the village," Mr. Duggleby said. "They see them in the marketplace. They say hello in the morning. They know exactly who they are."

In traditional Thailand, a hierarchy of power and position generally binds society. People know their place and offer due deference.

"For simple farmers to rise up against powerful people is really quite amazing, and daring," Mr. Duggleby said. "What it comes down to is, it's their village. There's a real sense of home, and where they were born and live is very important; for most people that's all they have."

https://lens.blogs.nytimes.com/2016/05/23/murdered-for-defending-thailands-environment/

My comments : totally unclear cause of death

Political murder (related to Karen ethnicity)

The Karen File

Ms Fatou Bensouda

Information and Evidence Unit

Office of the Prosecutor

Post Office Box 19519

2500 CM The Hague

The Netherlands

"

1 Who are the Karen ?

The Karen, Kayin, Kariang or Yang people (Karen: ကညီက
လၡ pronounced [kɲɔklɯ], Burmese: ကရင်လူမျို, pronounced [kəjɪ̀ɴ lù mjó]; Per Ploan
Poe or Ploan in Poe Karen and Pwa Ka Nyaw or Kanyaw in Sgaw Karen; Thai: กะเหรี่ยง or ยาง)
refer to a number of individual Sino-Tibetan language speaking ethnic groups, many of which do
not share a common language or culture. These Karen groups reside primarily in Karen State,
southern and southeastern Myanmar. The Karen make up approximately 7 percent of the total
Burmese population with approximately 5 million people.A large number of Karen have migrated
to Thailand, having settled mostly on the Thailand–Myanmar border.

(source Wikipedia …. https://en.wikipedia.org/wiki/Karen_people)

2 Life in the Refugee Camps

Around 400,000 Karen people are without housing, and 128,000 are living in camps on the
Thailand-Burma border. According to BMC, "79% of refugees living in these camps are Karen
ethnicity."Their lives are restricted in the camps because they usually cannot go out, and the Thai
police might arrest them if they do. Employment for the Karen refugees is scarce and risky. Former
refugee, Hla Wah, said, "No jobs..So if adults wanted to work, they had to leave quietly without
getting caught by Thai police." Wah is one of the Karen refugees who lived in a camp where she
went to school and helped her family because her parents sought to go out to work, but they
earned little money. Wah suffered from malnutrition because her parents did not have money to
buy food for her 9 siblings.

(source Wikipedia …. https://en.wikipedia.org/wiki/Karen_people)

3 The Karen Genocide in Burma

The Karen conflict is an ongoing armed conflict in Myanmar (Burma), and part of the bigger internal
conflict in Myanmar. The conflict has been described as one of the world's "longest running civil
wars".The Karen nationalist movement has been fighting for more autonomy and/or independence
within Burma.

The Karen people have been fighting for an independent Karen state since 1949, to Karen known
as Kawthoolei. In the sixty-year-long conflict many different actors have participated. The two most
influential actors were the Karen National Union(Burmese:ကရင် ၂ လ အစည်းabbreviated
KNU), a political organisation with an armed wing, the Karen National Liberation Army (KNLA) and
the Burmese Tatmadaw.

The conflict has mainly been fought in modern-day Karen state, which was established in 1952 by
the Burmese government. Only a minority of the total Karen population live within the borders of
this state. Hundreds of thousands of Karen and other ethnic groups have been killed in the conflict.

The conflict has also caused many Karen to flee Burma to Thailand.

The Karen people are one of the largest ethnic groups in Southeast Asia. The Karen constitute a population of 5-7 million and around twenty different Karen dialects are recognised of which Sgaw and Pwo Karen are the two most widely spoken. Other groups of Karen are the Kayah, Bwe, Kayan, Bre, Pa-o and some other subgroups.The Karen languages are part of the Tibeto-Burman languages which are a branch of the Sino-Tibetan languages.

It is generally agreed that the Karen began to arrive in what is today known as Burma around 500 BC. The Karen are believed to come from what is known today as Mongolia and travelled south through three river valleys: the Mekong Valley, the Irrawaddy Valley and the Salween valley. The Karen traditionally have five oral legends which explains their ancestry. The word 'Karen' is derived from different Tai and Burmese names for a collective term referring to people in the forest and in the mountains. The term Karen was never used by the people who are referred to by the term today. It was not until the nineteenth century that Christian missionaries from America and British colonial officers labelled these people 'Karen'.

The Karen are not an homogenous group. Different groups of Karen did not share the same history within the kingdoms of pre-colonial Burma or the British colonial empire. Some Karen fulfilled functions as ministers in urbanised kingdoms like the Pegu kingdom in the sixteenth century. Other Karen developed a subsistence way of living in the forests bordering Thailand and some Karen still practice this way of life. Around 20% of the Karen are Christian whereas 75% is Buddhists. A small percentage of Karen is animist and in the lowland riverdelta the so-called 'black Karen', a small minority, is Muslim. The Pwo speaking population constitutes around 80% of the total Karen population and they are mainly Buddhist. The speakers of Pwo Karen live in the plains of central and lower Burma and were assimilated into the dominant Mon social system throughout history. These 'Mon-Karen' or Talaing Kayin had a special status and were an essential part of Mon court life. The Bama Kayin or Sgaw Karen were either absorbed into Burmese society or pushed towards the mountains bordering Thailand in the east and Southeast of Burma by the Burmese population. The Karen living in Burma's eastern hills named the Dawna Range and the Tenasserim Hills bordering Thailand developed their own distinct society and history. The hill Karen communities developed a subsistence way of life.

Today about three million Karen live in the Irrawaddy river delta and they have developed an urbanised society based on the agriculture of rice. Karen communities are religiously, linguistically, culturally separated and geographyically dispersed. Some scholars have claimed 'the' Karen do not exist.

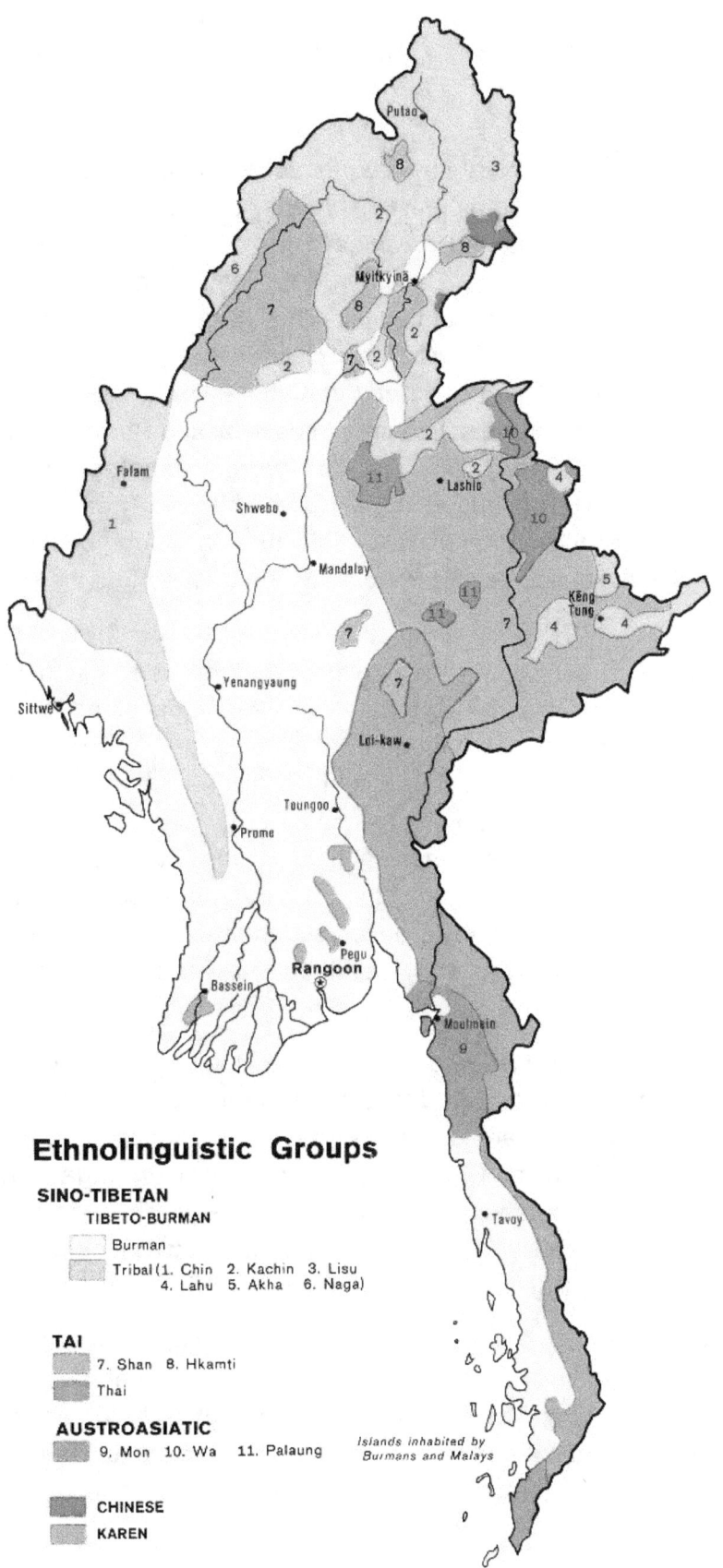

Ethnolinguistic Groups

SINO-TIBETAN

TIBETO-BURMAN

Burman

Tribal (1. Chin 2. Kachin 3. Lisu
4. Lahu 5. Akha 6. Naga)

TAI

7. Shan 8. Hkamti

Thai

AUSTROASIATIC

9. Mon 10. Wa 11. Palaung

Islands inhabited by Burmans and Malays

CHINESE

KAREN

4 Role of Thailand and the United States of America

The Thai government historically used Karen State as a buffer zone against the Burmese. After the Second World War the Thai were afraid of a communist insurgency developing from a union between Thai and Burmese communist, supported by China. Thus the Thai and US government supported Karen rebellions through the 1960s, 1970s and 1980s. The US government however also supported the Burmese government to fight communist. The US government provided weapons and American produced helicopters. The KNU has claimed that these weapons have been used against them.General Bo Mya once described the KNU as Thailands' 'foreign legion', because the KNU guarded the border the organisation prevented Thai and Burmese communist from unification. The strong shift to the right in 1976 under Bo Mya was a strategy to gain support from the Thai government.Thailands' policy changed in the 1990s when the Thai government started engaging its neighbours national government as equals. In 1997 Burma became a member of the ASEAN. The Thai government subsequently turned away from supporting the Karen armed groups.

The first Karen started to cross the border with Thailand in 1984 as a result from a major Four Cuts offensive by the Tatmadaw which lasted up to 1990.] By the mid-1990s tens of thousands of Karen refugees were living in camps along the Thai border. After the fall of Manerplawin 1995, 10,000 refugees crossed the border, most of them Karen. The Karen Conflict has been able to run for several decades because it has profited from being located in a border area. The introduction of the Burmese Way to Socialism helped to create a financial base for the KNU which has profited greatly from bordertrade with Thailand. The KNU levied taxes on in- and outgoing products. Besides that the KNU and other Karen armed groups have used the refugee camps in Thailand as sources for limited material support. KNU/KNLA family members received shelter in and supplies from the camps.

After the fall of Manerplaw in 1995, the KNU leadership has moved their headquarters to the border town of Mae Sot in Thailand. This has caused tension between the KNU leadership and the KNU officers on the ground within Burma. There is also disagreement amongst the Brigade leaders themselves, particularly between the Third and Fifth Brigades and the Fourth Brigade in the South, in the Tenasserim region. The Tatmadaw opened a new offensive in 1997. This again resulted in a new stream of Karen refugees towards Thailand. The border at Mae Sot was closed for a short period in 2010 because of rising tensions between the KNU and the DKBA.

The organisational structure of the KNU was so successful it has been copied by other insurgent groups in Burma. Each unit of the KNU was self-supporting. Not only the armed units, but also the hospitals and schools were self-supporting. The strength of this strategy is that it is hard to erase such a movement since it is very spread out and lacks a centre. The weakness and disadvantage of the KNU has been that KNU units had trouble getting help from their neighbouring KNU units.

5 **Refugees**

At least two million people of many different ethnic groups are internally displaced in Burma. Another two million ethnic minorities from Burma have found refuge in neighbouring countries. A large portion of this latter group is Karen. The first Karen refugees started to arrive in Thailand in 1984.The KNU has greatly benefited from the refugee camps in Thailand. The KNU has used these camps as safehavens and has been provided with food and other materials through family members and friends who stayed in the camps. Around two hundred thousand Karen and Karenni are placed in nine refugee camps within Thailand on the Thai-Burma Border.Since 2006 a resettlement program has been set up. 73,775 Karen people were resettled in July 2011 to mostly Western countries, predominantly the United States of America. In January 2011 the Thai Burmese Border Consortium (TBBC) set the total number of refugees at 141,549 people.

6 **Conflict since 2000**

The Karen split up into many different armed units after the 1990s. The Karen National Union (KNU) was heavily weakened after this decade. In 2004 substantial ceasefire talks were held again between Gen. Bo Mya and Burmese general Khin Nyunt. Unfortunately Khin Nyunt was expulsed from the government. In 2005 two more peace talks were held, but it was clear that the new government under the leadership of Than Shwe was not interested in establishing a ceasefire. In 2006 the long-term leader and Second World War veteran General Bo Mya died. Old time general-secretary of the KNU, Padoh Mahn Sha Lah Phan took over Bo Mya's function. Padoh Mahn Sha was important for the political relations and the reorganisation of the KNU. However, on 14 February 2008 he was assassinated. In 2007 Major General Htin Maung left with a sizeable portion of the KNLA Seventh Brigade. This group now calls themselves KNU-KNLA Peace Council. If further decimated the strength and influence of the KNU.

On 20 March 2010, 2 people were killed and 11 were wounded in a blast on a bus in Karen state.

In November 2010 the Thailand-Burma border areas saw an upsurge in fighting following elections in November 2010. Twenty thousand people fled over the border to Thailand in November 2010. For the first time in fifteen years the KNU and the DKBA were united to fight the Tatmadaw. But as of early 2011 the KNU is only one in seven Karen armed factions that is active in fighting. The KNU barely holds any territory inside Burma and the future of the organisation and the Karen struggle for independence is uncertain.An initial ceasefire was reached on 12 January 2012 in Hpa-an and fighting has stopped in nearly all Karen State.

6 Summary

At this moment approximately 150,000 Karen people live inside refugee camps or concentration camps in Thailand close to the border with Myanmar. A return to Myanmar is possible but the persecution by the Burmese and the Karen-Burmese war have not ended. A safe return to Myanmar is an illusion, and at the same time is a longer stay in the concentration camps equally harsh ...

The Thai immigration Act and Nationality Act do not permit any of the Karen people to easily obtain Thai nationality, not even after 40 years in the concentration camps – refugee camps. Their legal status is non-existent. Neither Burma nor Thailand recognize these people, they are stateless ...

8 Condition inside the concentration camps

The Thai government has allowed the Karen to live in small villages ... they have to build their housing themselves, electricity and water are scarce ... health care is distant and food is equally rationed ... The Thai government at least provides some help, just enough for the Karen people to survive ... however the suicide rate in these camps is extremely high.

The Karen allowed to live in the camps and can wander a few kilometers around the villages ... however at any given moment, inside the camps and outside Karen can be arrested as illegal aliens and deported to Myanmar ... The Thai government does not really want to arrest the Karen as sending them back could lead to additional costs ... so the Karen in Thailand are left to themselves and have to try to have a more or less decent life without any help at all ....

Young women go to Bangkok, Pattaya, Phuket but as they have no legal status and no real paperwork end up in human trafficking or slavery ...

Below a report by Burma Link.

https://www.burmalink.org/background/thailand-burma-border/displaced-in-thailand/refugee-camps/

Many people around the world take for granted the freedom to travel and freedom to work. Others have learned to take for granted that they are unable to do so. Thousands of refugees from Burma have lived confined to the camps in Thailand for 30 years. Although refugee camps are hardly natural places to live, thousands have been born in the camps and never left. For the vast majority of them, the only way of life they have ever known is one forced to be dependent on outside assistance. For many young refugees, refugee camps are where they were born and where they grew up, and the only reality they have ever seen exists within the fences of the camp.

> *"It is so strict to live here. There is nothing to do. I am not allowed to go outside the camp. There is no job, no work. So much stress and depression. I feel that I am going to go crazy here." (Burmese refugee, Nu Po camp, Tak province, January 2012; Human Rights Watch, 2012e, p. 18)*

Meanwhile, many older people have lived in the camps for so long that they can hardly remember their homeland anymore. This is all the while the refugee camps are only considered "temporary shelters" by Thai authorities who can close down the camps whenever they decide to do so. Thailand, in recent years, has made it no secret that they want to close the camps, causing growing concerns among the refugee population who do not feel safe to return.

When the first refugees arrived in 1984, no one could have ever predicted that only would they still be there 30 years on. Majority of the refugees in the camps are Karen (79.1%) or Karenni

(10.3%) from eastern Burma (TBC, December, 2014), who have fled armed conflicts and/or horrendous human rights abuse and persecution by the Burmese military. The government policy of Four Cuts, and what has been described as the slow genocide of ethnic peoples (La Guardia, June, 2005), resulted in the widespread destruction of communities and the decline of traditional cultures. Thousands of villages, especially in the Karen and Karenni States, were burned to the ground, including houses, religious buildings, schools, belongings, and sometimes even domestic animals. In many areas, it became the norm for the villagers to live in a constant fear of the Burmese military coming to their village, terrorising the villagers, stealing their food, forcing villagers to become porters and mine sweepers, raping ethnic women, and torturing and killing anyone suspected of having a connection the ethnic armed opposition. Whilst some villagers endured the abuse by developing warning systems and repeatedly fleeing to the jungle, others, who had heard about Thailand, decided to leave their village for good. Others still had no choice as their village was already in ashes on the ground.

Until 1995, refugees on the Thailand-Burma border lived in village-type settlements and were allowed to travel outside the camps to get food and shelter materials. Camp life changed dramatically in 1995 after the DKBA attacks; the village-type settlements were merged into large, sprawling camps that became increasingly dependent on outside aid as residents became more and more restricted on space and movement (TBC, 2004). Refugees still frequently break the rules of confinement and as a consequence, are often detained and occasionally deported (e.g. SHRF & SWAN, 2002). There are even reports of refugees been found killed outside the camp fences under mysterious circumstances (see e.g. Human Rights Watch, 2012e, pp. 37-38; Poe Kwa Lay, November 2012). Refugees have no means of seeking redress; similarly to Burmese authorities in their home country, Thai officials often seem to enjoy total impunity (see Human Rights Watch, 2012e).

Throughout the 1980s, 1990s, and 2000s, more refugees kept pouring across the border to Thailand. Alongside the growing need, a humanitarian and human rights network grew along the border. One of the organisations to respond to the crisis is The Border Consortium (TBC), which remains the main agency organising food and other aid to the refugees. TBC was originally formed by TBC's former Executive Director Jack Dundorf who was among the first people to witness and respond to the urgent needs of thousands of refugees who fled to Thailand in 1984. TBC gradually evolved into a multi-membership aid organisation, and is one of the Executive Members of the Committee for Coordination of Services to Displaced Persons in Thailand (CCSDPT) that works together with the UNHCR to coordinate all humanitarian service and protection activities in Thailand.

TBC maintains a database which includes all registered and unregistered refugees and is shared with the UNHCR to ensure compatibility. The database is updated monthly for births, deaths, departures, and new arrivals, to create the 'verified caseload'. Food rations are distributed only to those who show up in person to receive their supplies. The actual number of people fed each month is known as the "feeding figure." According to the December 2014 figures, the verified caseload in the camps was 110,607 and the feeding figure 108,583. As nearly 100,000 have been resettled to third countries, current numbers do not represent the overall population that has fled to the camps over the years.

In the camps, refugees have limited educational and training opportunities and no official means of earning an income. While education in the camps is far better than any education available to civilians inside Burma, there are limited opportunities for higher education, which also largely remains unrecognised outside the camps. Karen and other ethnic peoples of Burma traditionally place a very high value on education and many have crossed the border to Thailand in order to go to a camp school. Although the majority of the camp populations have arrived as a family unit (TBC, 2012b), many parents also send their children to attend schools in refugee camps across the Thai border (KHRG, 2008).

"If we had stayed in the village, we knew that our children could never attend school and I wanted my children to go to school to be educated people. We also didn't have any house to stay in. We could only stay in the forest and we had to flee away when the SPDC came or patrolled around our area, so we decided it was better to go to the refugee camp." (Saw P—, a 47-year-old male from P— village, Papun District; KHRG, 2008, p. 58)

With more than 40,000 residents, Mae La is the biggest of the refugee camps on the Thailand-Burma border. Due to its size and easily accessibly location, Mae La is considered a centre of study for refugees. Mae La's current population includes 1,039 boarding house students who have come to study in the camp mostly from Burma. In total, as of July 2014 there were 2,763 boarding house students in the camps (TBC, 2014a). Many other students also stay with their relatives in the camps. The issue for many young students is what happens after they finish a post-ten school, the highest level of education available in most of the camps. There are only a handful of schools on the Thailand-Burma border where these young students can apply for, leaving thousands of talented and dedicated aspiring university students with no means to educate themselves.

Education in the camps is provided by CBOs such as the Karen Refugee Committee – Education Entity (KRC-EE) backed up by international NGOs such as World Education. Many schools, especially in the less remote camps in Tak Province, have foreign teachers and volunteers, majority of whom stay illegally in the camps as permits remain largely unattainable. These foreigners teach refugees English and other subjects while hiding from Thai authorities, risking fines or even deportation. After the Thai junta took over power in May 2014, however, it has become increasingly difficult to enter and stay in the camps without a permit.

Educational opportunities also vary greatly from one camp to the next. In the more remote camps such as Mae La Oon in Mae Hong Son Province and Ban Don Yang in Kanchanaburi Province, situation is dire as education remains largely unattainable, and higher education institutions are far away out of reach. Most of these opportunities are available either in the Tak camps – Mae La, Umpiem Mai and Nu Po – or in the border town of Mae Sot.

One of the most prestigious of the schools available for refugees is the Australian Catholic University (ACU), which offers a Diploma in Liberal Studies in Mae Sot as well as in Ranong. Other commendable schools include the Wide Horizons and Minmahaw GED Programs in Mae

Sot, English Immersion Program in Umpiem Mai, and Global Border Studies Program in Nu Po. As these opportunities are only available to a few students each year, thousands of capable young adults are left with no means to pursue their dream of higher education. Many young people are determined to help their people and their country, but with no place to go for study, they often end up opening a shop or becoming a nurse or a teacher in the camp. Some leave to find factory work in Bangkok or elsewhere in Thailand while many others turn to drugs and alcohol, or even commit suicide, as they see their dreams crushed before them.

Having lived in a place where freedom of movement as well as self-expression is severely restricted, many young refugees feel scared about leaving the refugee camps even to pursue higher education in other camps on the border. Most have heard stories about the police check points and intimidation by Thai authorities that sometimes takes place even when refugees have managed to obtain travel documents (Human Rights Watch, 2012e). Others have already experienced being thrown to a detention centre and are reluctant to take the risk of leaving the camps.

International organisations such as the UNHCR, the United Nations Children's Fund (UNICEF) and the International Committee of the Red Cross (ICRC) have also faced restrictions in Thailand that have made it difficult for them to provide even rudimentary protection for those who have crossed the border to Thailand (see Human Rights Watch, 2007). The framework of international principles that recognises the inherent dignity and the equal and inalienable rights of all members of the human family to be universally protected have little significance to refugees who live in Thailand.

The 1951 United Nations Convention lays down basic minimum standards for the treatment of refugees, including access to the courts, to primary education, and to work (UNHCR, 2010). The Convention defines a refugee as a person who:

> *"…owing to well-founded fear of being persecuted for reasons of race, religion, nationality, membership of a particular social group or political opinion, is outside the country of his nationality and is unable or, owing to such fear, is unwilling to avail himself of the protection of that country; or who, not having a nationality and being outside the country of his former habitual residence as a result of such events, is unable or, owing to such fear, is unwilling to return to it."*

Thailand is not a party to the 1951 Convention or its 1967 Protocol. For 30 years now, Thailand's policy has been to confine the 'persons of concern' to their 'temporary shelters' until the situation in Burma would improve and the displaced could go home. The Burmese government has also consistently denied having any problems associated with refugees. In 2003, the government published a highly controversial statement:

"As Myanmar is not engaged in any war with other countries, there is no problem of refugees. The armed insurrection groups also have come back into the legal fold and there is peace in the country." (Government of Burma, 2003, p. 54, IX A art.22 / 217)

While the UNHCR publically maintains that "…the generosity of the Royal Thai Government in hosting refugees and asylum-seekers has spanned several decades" (UNHCR, 2012b), others have described Thailand's refugee policies as "fragmented, unpredictable, inadequate and ad hoc (e.g. Human Rights Watch, 2012e, p. 1)." Even UNHCR goes on to explain how they operate in a challenging environment, which is characterised by inadequate protection space for many persons of concern. Although UNHCR normally promotes three durable solutions for refugees; repatriation to their home countries, local integration in the host country, or resettlement to third countries, none of these solutions were available in Thailand until 2004 (TBC, 2012b), twenty years after the first refugees had arrived from Burma.

Thai authorities allowed refugees to register with the UNHCR periodically during 2004 and 2005, and since 2005, all registered refugees have been eligible for resettlement to third countries. In June 2014, 96,206 had been resettled, vast majority (75%) of them to the US, followed by Australia, Canada, Finland, and Norway (TBC, 2014a). Departures for resettlement have declined each year since 2008, mainly because the majority of those who were able to register in 2004 and 2005 have already left. The group settlement program to the US has now closed, but a significant number remain in the pipeline and are expected to depart in 2015 (TBC, 2014a).

Of the current camp residents, 33.5% are not registered and thus ineligible for resettlement (TBC, 2015a). Refugees also have numerous concerns regarding resettlement that often lead to eligible refugees staying in the camps. One of the common issues is the inability to organise family reunions when resettled refugees have children that are over the age of 18. Those who have been resettled often have done so in order to provide for their families and relatives in the camps. Refugees typically maintain close links with the camps and frequently send money to their loved ones. According to Human Rights Watch (2012e), despite the UNHCR having a presence on the border since 1998, its role in the camps is extremely limited. Human Rights Watch adds: "The agency has demonstrated little ability to counter the Thai government's ad hoc policies of containment and provides virtually no protection to Burmese asylum seekers outside the camps (p. 19)."

As a result of inadequate protection of refugees, as well as the highly restricted life in the camps, thousands live in the country as illegal aliens (for more information, see **In Exile Outside the Camps**). Many Burman nationals who have fled their home country, including most former (forcibly conscripted) child soldiers in the Burma army, also remain outside the refugee camps because they fear they may be ostracised by the refugee population who has fled Burmese military (most of whom are Burman) abuses and who are usually of a different ethnicity. Many Burman refugees in the camps talk about problems of discrimination, exclusion, and suspicions of being government spies, often leading them to depart the camps in the end. Other camp residents, who speak Burmese, have also faced similar problems as they have been mistaken for being Burman. Refugees belonging to minority groups, however, say that the situation has improved in recent years and refugees are mostly not afraid to speak Burmese anymore.

Due to the refugees in the camps being forced to be nearly completely dependent on outside help for food, shelter, protection and other basic needs, their coping mechanisms have been severely eroded. Travel and work restrictions have had adverse psychological and social effects on the refugees, decreasing their self-sufficiency, camp morale and mental health (TBC, 2012b).

> *"Living in the camp is similar to living in prison because I can't go outside or make my own decision. I can commute only in the camp. The camp is surrounded by barbed wire. If we go outside of the camp, Thai police will arrest us. In the long run, it affects not only my physical but also my mental health." (Christine, 22, Karen refugee, spoke with Burma Link in Mae La refugee camp in May 2014; see 'Authorities Should Take Action for Refugees NOW')*

In a 2006 study, PU-AMI found that 50% of adult camp residents suffer from mental health problems and anti-depressants constituted one of the most common drug prescriptions for refugees (as cited in Human Rights Watch, 2012e, p. 19). Halting long-term sustainability prospects in the camps has also created a climate where refugees tend to think only short-term, from one ration to another. Some refugees have adapted this form of thinking already back in Burma where many were forced to flee Burma Army attacks from one hiding site to another. When the refugees will eventually return to Burma, many of them will need assistance not only in skills to sustain themselves but also in changing their thinking from short-term survival to long-term development. In a similar vein, those who have remained in hiding inside the country have been on the run for so long that many consider it normal to regularly flee and hide from government forces and to build a new village after another.

Considering the often traumatic backgrounds as well as the challenging circumstances that refugees face in Thailand, many people who visit the camps are impressed by the significant effort refugees make in order to maintain dignity and hope in the camp communities. Despite severe restrictions and depressive realities, refugees strive to remain active and to maintain their cultural traditions through practices such as teaching ethnic nationality languages and dances. People marry and have children, play sports, and organise festivals and other celebrations. Despite the devastating reality, life goes on. Thousands of people of Burma have come to consider these enclosed areas as their homes, trying to lead their lives as the best they can.

"From the beginning I was moved by the faith and dignity of the refugees I met, their determination to get on with their lives as best as they could, and their apparent belief that somehow, someday, justice would be done." (Jack Dunford, Executive Director of TBC 1984-2012; TBC, 2013a)£

While vast majority of refugees in the camps are ethnic Karen from eastern Burma, camps also vary greatly with regard to ethnic diversity. Umpiem Mai and Nu Po are the most ethnically diverse with over 20% of the camp populations comprising of non-Karen or Karenni ethnic groups. Mae Ra Ma Luang, Mae La Oon, and Tham Hin are the most homogenous with ethnic

Karen comprising 99% of the populations (TBC, 2013c). Literacy rate in the camps is estimated as 60% (TBC, 2013c).

When living in the camps, one will notice the integral part that religion plays in most refugees' lives. Religious buildings are centres of communal activities and refugees regularly attend religious ceremonies, sing and listen to religious songs, and read religious texts. Prayers are said before each meal, and often before the beginning of each school day. Most refugees are either Christian (51%) or Buddhist (36%), which is evident in the way refugees often ask visitors whether they are Christian or Buddhist, as if there are no other religions. In the Tak camps, however, there are also significant Muslim communities. Muslims have been particularly successful in setting up businesses in the camps, particularly noticeable in Mae La camp, where the main market has only one shop maintained by an ethnic Karen, the rest being run by Muslims.

Most of the camps are isolated in the mountains and at the end of dirt roads, while some camps, such as Mae La and Umpiem Mai, are located as close as 1 to 1.5 hour drive away from the nearest town of Mae Sot. The isolated camps tend to be far away from hospitals and some of them have no phone signal (Human Rights Watch, 2012e). The realities in the remote camps are very different from the easily accessible camps that also have much more opportunities for study and work. In these camps almost all residents are de facto refugees, as the camps have had very little pull factor other than safety from the Burmese military.

Three of the camps (Mae La, Tham Hin, and Ban Don Yang) are overcrowded (Human Rights Watch, 2012e). In all camps, the challenge of space is a significant concern. When living in one of the camps one will notice the almost complete lack of personal space or privacy. In some areas of the camps, houses are built right next to each other, people are everywhere, and it seems to never be quiet as there is always someone in the earshot singing, playing music, listening to the radio, or simply talking. Refugees who still have memories of life in Burma struggle to adapt to having no space around their houses; "Here, it is like fifty villages are crammed into one," one refugee told TBC (2004, p. 53).

Due to space restrictions and limited housing supplies provided in the camps, many households comprise more than one family and young married couples typically continue to live with their parents. Space restrictions coupled with bamboo building materials also make camps into 'fire traps' and despite refugees being aware of the danger, fires regularly sweep through the communities. In February 2012, a huge fire in Umpiem camp destroyed as many as 1,000 houses (Karen News, February, 2012). In April 2013, 36 refugees died in a tragic fire that destroyed Ban Mae Surin refugee camp in Mae Hong Son Province. In December 2013, around 750 refugees were left homeless in Mae La camp when more than a hundred houses were destroyed by a fire. The next day one refugee woman died in a fire in Ban Mai Nai Soi camp.

Although some basic health care is provided in the camps, diseases such as malaria, dengue fever and tuberculosis are still common among the refugees. According to TBC (2015a), the border-wide average chronic (stunting) malnutrition rate is classified as "very high", with camps with the highest stunting rates being located in the most remote areas of the border.

The camps are highly organised with regularly elected camp leaders, committees, and section leaders, although refugees regularly complain about corruption and lack of transparency in the leadership. The Karen Refugee Committee (KRC) and the Karenni Refugee Committee (KnRC) are the overall representatives of the refugees living in the camps. These Committees coordinate and oversee all camp activities through the Camp Committees, coordinate assistance provided by NGOs, and liaise with UNHCR, Thai authorities, and security personnel (TBC, 2013a). Each camp is headed by a single leader and hundreds of people serve on the Camp Committees, organising the storage and distribution of rations, safeguarding the camps' physical environment and infrastructure, and overseeing health clinics, the school system, and the administration of justice (TBC, 2004).

The latest Refugee Committee and Camp Committee elections were held in early 2013. According to TBC (2013a), all registered and unregistered refugees over the age of 20, regardless of gender, religion and ethnicity, were able to vote. Camp residents, however, voiced concerns over the elections. According to one young refugee who spoke with Burma Link, "Most people don't know whether they are eligible to vote or not. So, most unregistered didn't vote".

A variety of CBOs formed by members of the refugee communities also support specific social groups, such as the Karenni Students Union, the Karen Youth Organisation, and the Karen Handicapped Welfare Association. Refugee women's organisations have also actively sought ways to improve women's participation in all aspects of society.

TBC remains the only agency responsible for providing food and shelter assistance to the refugees in the camps. In the past, TBC also regularly purchased and distributed blankets, mosquito nets, clothing for children under five and thread for longyi weaving, sleeping mats, and cooking pots both to current and newly arrived camp residents. Recent funding cuts on the border have forced TBC to cease the provision of all non-food items even to new arrivals. Only cooking stoves and donated items are still being distributed to refugees. As a consequence of the funding cuts, TBC's food rations have also fallen substantially below minimum daily nutritional levels (see TBC, 2013a, p. 44). Health and education services for the refugees have also been cut back, having an adverse effect on the camp residents.

As the recent restrictions in movement have strictly prohibited refugees from leaving camp premises, the reduced rations have become a grave concern. According to the refugees themselves, it is the poorest and the most vulnerable who suffer the consequences as they are not able to go to the forest to hunt for rats and collect vegetables, nor to buy extra food as they are now not allowed to take on work as daily workers. Some refugees are now employing more risky behaviours and strategies in order to bridge the widened gap between their basic needs and the humanitarian assistance they receive. While some households are able to supplement their needs through well-established economic activities, others are simply no longer able to meet their basic needs.

In order to cope with the situation, TBC has employed a method of identifying food secure and insecure households in order to implement Community Managed Targeting, in which self-reliant refugees will forfeit their rations whilst the most vulnerable receive extra supplies (see TBC, 2013a, p. 45). Eye-witness accounts, however, tell a grim story as Burma Link has received reports of some refugees believing they are being starved out in order to avoid their continuing assistance and future repatriation.

Many refugees refuse to settle for their faith as helpless and passive victims and are making great efforts to cope and provide for their families through taking part in different livelihood activities, when possible. Some international NGOs and local CBOs such as TBC provide the refugees with opportunities for skills training and income generation, although these projects reach only a small part of refugee populations. Refugees are also often left frustrated as after taking part in the training, they have nowhere to use their newly-found skills. Some have taken part in one TBC training after another, unable to apply their skills in practice.

TBC does, however, have several successful projects in the camps such as the Community Agriculture Program (CAP) that is currently implemented in eight camps (TBC, 2014a). CAP gardening activities are important in that they increase the availability of fresh food in camps, and prepare refugees with vital livelihood skills. As a result of CAP activities, hundreds of households in the camps are now able to cultivate their own gardens. TBC also supports some projects run by local CBOs on Burma side of the border, e.g. the Back Pack Health Worker Team's (BPHWT) water supply and sanitation projects and the Karen Human Rights Group's (KHRG's) village agency project.

Other organisations also undertake training activities in the camps. COERR, for example, has trained refugees on appropriate and sustainable organic agricultural practices, assisted refugee communities to develop basic social work technical skills, and provided vocational training for individuals in extremely vulnerable situations (see COERR – Project).

These activities, when successfully implemented, are essential for the refugees to regain confidence, motivation, and a sense of independence from external aid. They will also be extremely valuable for refugees if they return to Burma or are resettled in third countries. Since 2005, the UNHCR and CCSDPT have advocated with the Thai authorities for a relaxation in the policy of confinement to camps (see TBC, 2013a). The policy nevertheless remains in place and restrictions have recently been tightened. While many refugees make significant efforts to remain active in the challenging and often depressive situation, the vast majority of camp residents are increasingly reliant on outside support and aid as a result of forced passivity.

The recent political changes and ceasefire talks in Burma have resulted in widespread and grossly premature talks of repatriating the refugees. Only one month after Burma transitioned to a nominally civilian government in March 2011, Thai authorities announced that they are in the process of discussion with the Burmese government about closing the refugee camps (Chitradon, April, 2011). More recently, the Thai junta announced that it wants to repatriate all refugees by 2015 (Saw Yan Naing, July, 2014b). These are grave concerns for the refugees as major obstacles for safe repatriation remain. In fact, none of the reasons why refugees fled have seen a sustainable solution; peace process has stalled, ceasefires remain fragile and unpredictable, landmines contamination is among the worst in the world, health and education is lacking, poverty is rampant, and human rights violations continue (see e.g. Davis, Gittleman, Sollom, Richards, & Beyrer, 2012; KHRG, 2014a; ND-Burma, 2013b, 2014a, 2014b).

Although the consensus is that conditions are not yet conducive for refugees to return, there are now significant concerns that camps could be closed and refugees repatriated before they can do so with a sense of dignity and hope. In recent years, even TBC has changed their focus to preparedness for refugee and IDP return (TBC, 2013a, 2014a). Talks about repatriation coupled with reduced aid and increased restrictions have caused anxiety and uncertainty among the refugees who do not feel safe returning to their homeland. Despite the positive change that has emerged during the past years, much more needs to be done before refugees can safely return to Burma yet no one knows when the refugees will have to go back and whether they can do so voluntarily.

It is hoped that organisations such as the TBC and UNHCR, as well as the international donor community, will be willing to continue necessary support on the border until the time is right for refugees to return. A major current challenge, however, is that many NGOs and CBOs along the border are struggling to sustain even basic services to refugees as donors are shifting their funds inside Burma. One can only hope that agencies such as the UNHCR will respect its public commitments and "ensure that repatriation is voluntary, undertaken in safety and dignity, and takes place only when conditions are conducive" (UNHCR, 2013b).

T he recent political changes and ceasefires in Burma have resulted in widespread and grossly premature talks of refugee repatriation. Although the consensus is that conditions are not yet conducive for refugees to return, there are now significant concerns that refugee camps on the Thailand-Burma border could be closed and refugees repatriated before they can do so with a sense of dignity and hope.

> *"Our main need is security. We want the Burmese soldiers out of our area, and take the landmines they planted out too. When we return, we don't want the Burmese soldiers harassing us again." (Karen man, CIDKP focus group, Palaw Township, interviewed in June 2008; TBC, 2008, p. 14)*

Talks about repatriation coupled with reduced aid have caused anxiety among the camp communities as most refugees do not feel safe returning to their homeland. Thailand has issued repeated threats to send refugees back to Burma (see e.g. Saw Yan Naing, September, 2012) and to close down the camps (Chitradon, April 2011; Saw Yan Naing, July, 2014b). This is a significant concern as formidable obstacles for safe repatriation, including the ongoing human rights violations in ethnic border areas as well as widespread landmine contamination, still remain, and genuine and lasting peace is yet nowhere in sight.

It is also worrying that both Thai authorities and the UNHCR have forcibly returned refugees back to Burma in the past despite grave ongoing human rights violations. In 1995, UNHCR "voluntarily" repatriated over 200,000 Burmese refugees from Bangladesh, most of them Rohingya. In 1996, at least 10,000 refugees attempted a desperate return to Bangladesh where the UNHCR was now denied any operational role. At least 15 women and young children drowned to death. As pointed out by the Human Rights Watch (1996); "The 1996 exodus from Burma raises several important questions about the UNHCR's repatriation operation from Bangladesh and about the promotion of "voluntary" return to countries with particularly abusive governments." The UNHCR also acknowledged the issue:

> "…in some instances UNHCR has placed too much emphasis on early return to countries of origin which has resulted in return movements to less than favourable conditions." (UNHCR, Oslo Declaration and Plan of Action, June 1994, as cited in Human Rights Watch, 1996).

According to the Arakanese National Rohingya Organization (ARNO), many more refugees also lost their lives over the years whilst resisting forced repatriation from Bangladesh to Burma (ARNO, 2012).

In 1996, Thailand forced Mon refugees near Sangkhlaburi to go back to Burma following a ceasefire signed between the New Mon State party (NMSP) and the Burmese government. After been forcibly repatriated, these Mon refugees remained far from their original homeland, received inadequate aid, and were unable to support themselves, according to the TBC (2004). The ceasefire did not lead to political dialogue, as none of them have, and subsequently broke in 2010. A new ceasefire was signed again 2012, but similarly to all the numerous ceasefires signed between the government and ethnic armies since the 1990s, the government has made no indication of actually discussing the possibility of establishing a federal union. As long as the government refuses to discuss the political goals of the ethnic organisations, all ceasefires are bound to be broken.

Thousands are now holding their breath praying that the past mistakes by the UNHCR and the Thai government will not be repeated in the Karen and Karenni camps on the Thailand-Burma border. Despite the positive change that has emerged under the Thein Sein administration, much more needs to be done before lasting peace and security can become a reality. Repatriation should arguably be a refugee-led voluntary operation and not enforced by outside actors.

> "I don't think you really need to return refugees back because if conditions were right, the refugees would go back of their own free will". (Aung San Suu Kyi on June 2, 2012; Burma Partnership short documentary highlighting refugees' voices about repatriation from camps along the Thailand border back into Burma: "**Nothing About Us Without Us**")

Furthermore, there are also significant concerns that refugees and local CBOs have been left out of the repatriation planning. The key to successful return will not only be that it is voluntary but also that community participation is guaranteed in all stages of the preparedness and planning process.

> *"The refugees and internally displaced people are part of the solution, not the problem, and we all pray that before long they will be able to go back to Burma/Myanmar and play an important role in helping build a modern and peaceful nation." (Jack Dunford, Executive Director of TBC 1984-2012; TBC, 2013)*

On their website, the UNHCR (2013b) listed as one of their targets and objectives for 2013 in Thailand that, "All persons of concern in the nine camps have access to information on conditions in potential return areas in Myanmar (Burma) and on basic protection standards regarding voluntary repatriation." At the same time, there seemed to be no public information on where the refugees would go and refugees themselves seemed utterly unaware of anything related to the repatriation planning (based on Burma Link's interviews with refugees in September 2012, March 2013, November 2013, December 2014, and January 2015). The situation seems largely the same today, and by January 2015, the UNHCR had removed this target from their website (UNHCR, 2015).

In March 2013, the KRC issued a statement outlining ten points to repatriation, including a nationwide ceasefire, settling of political conflicts, and respect for universal human rights (Karen News, March, 2013). The KRC said again in May 2013 that it wants refugees to return only after the building of a genuine peace between the government and the KNU, and that when it is time to implement repatriation, all refugees should be returned at the same time and not as part of a "repatriation pilot" as suggested by the Burmese government (Saw Khar Su Nyar, May, 2013).

In May and June 2013, refugees' fears of premature repatriation were fuelled following a UN-led profiling survey. Burma Link came across significant unheard refugee concerns as more than 3,600 refugees in Mae La camp had signed a petition refusing to participate in the survey, claiming the questionnaire solicited answers that favour repatriation (Sullivan, June, 2013). The refugees feared that the information could be used as an indication of "voluntary return" and demanded that the survey be re-authored with their participation and approval. The petition was delivered to the UNHCR and an article about the issue was published on the Democratic Voice of Burma (see Sullivan, June, 2013). Although the survey never got refugees' approval, it saw some important changes; refugees now needed to rank a preference of minimum two options for their future, instead of three (which meant they no longer had to indicate that going back to Burma is one of the choices they voluntarily choose for their future – read also Burma Link's interview with the refugee who led the petition). The profiling survey has now been conducted in all camps along the border.

Refugees still remained sceptical about the underlying motives of the survey and the fact that it was conducted with tablets. One young refugee woman, Christine, told Burma Link in May 2014 that "even though we say the real answer, they [/fusion_builder_column]

[Mae Fa Luang Foundation, a Thai NGO that was subcontracted to conduct the survey] can change it later by themselves (Burma Link, 2014b)."

After the Thai military took over power in a coup in May, 2014, refugees' concerns and fears have grown even more. The junta has significantly restricted refugees' movement, announced that all refugees will be repatriated in 2015, and conducted a head count in the camps (see e.g. Saw Yan Naing, July, 2014a, 2014b). Thai authorities have given very little details of their repatriation plans or the underlying reasons for the head count. The UNHCR has also recently started their own headcount in the camps, which most refugees think will give them a chance to register as refugees and be resettled. Although the UNHCR has announced that the headcount is not be an official registration, the refugees have little faith in the organisation telling them the truth; most think this is their last chance to get out and start a new life.

> *"We don't know when they will close the camp, or when they close the camp, where we should go. We don't know… if authorities arrange forced repatriation, refugees will refuse to go back and it can build tension between refugees and authorities." (Christine, 22, Karen refugee, spoke with Burma Link in Mae La refugee camp in May 2014; see 'Authorities Should Take Action for Refugees NOW')*

Currently none of the original reasons why refugees fled have been sustainably resolved, and it is imperative that the refugees are not forced, directly or indirectly, to go back to the country that they so desperately escaped from.

8 Legal status

With the present Immigration Act of Thailand, the Karen have no legal status in Thailand, they can not own land ... the jobs available for them are extremely limited ... By not signing the Refugee Convention, Thailand also has declared that "genocide" does not exist and is "no excuse" for becoming a refugee .... However Thailand signed the Convention against Torture and meets all the conditions for breaches of this convention by making life as hard as possible for these illegal aliens ...

In the "official" press the Royal Thai Government explains it takes care of the Karen and helps them go home, where they either blow themselves up on land mines or are subjected to the genocidal ultra – nationalistic regime of the Burmese generals.

However ....

All over the world and also in Thailand people have been speaking up for the Karen ...

9 Political assassinations connected to the Karen refugee situation

a) Porlajee Rakchongcharoen, who was called Billy, was last seen at a national park checkpoint on April 17, 2014, after he was detained for apparently illegally collecting wild honey in the forest. He was a leader in the Karen community living in Kaeng Krachan National Park. He had filed a lawsuit against park officials over the destruction and burning of houses of over 20 Karen families in the national park's Pong Luk Bang Kloy villages.

b) Kampan Suksai was shot and killed on Dec. 20, 2003, on the main road in Pa Ngam village in Chiang Mai Province. He was a village leader who opposed encroachment in a community forest. The gunman was imprisoned but has been released.
(related to Karen People – Hill Tribes)

c) Supol Sirijant, 58, was shot and killed in his home on Aug. 11, 2004. As the leader of the Mae Mok Community Forestry Network, in the Toen District of Lampang Province, he fought the illegal logging of a nearby community forest.
(related to Karen People – Hill Tribes)

d) February 14, 2005, Karen National Union leader Mahn Sha who, was gunned down at his home in the Thai border town of Mae Sot.

The Police investigation is still going on.

e) there are many more ....